THE INSPIRING JOURNEY OF
CHRISTIANO RONALDO

The story of Hard Work Determination and Success

Michael E. Nichols

Copyright © 2024 by Michael E. Nichols

All Rights Reserved.

No part of this book may be used or reproduced by any means, graphic, electronic, or mechanical, including photocopying, recording, taping, or by any information storage retrieval system without the written permission of the Author.

TABLE OF CONTENTS

CHAPTER 1:   Early Life and Childhood

CHAPTER 2:   Rise to Stardom: Sporting Lisbon Days

CHAPTER 3:   Manchester United: The Making of a Global Icon

CHAPTER 4   : European Glory: Champions League Success

CHAPTER 5:   International Career: Portugal's Golden Boy

CHAPTER 6:   Real Madrid Era: Records and Rivalries

CHAPTER 7:   Ballon d'Or Dominance: Individual Accolades

CHAPTER 8:   Transfer to Juventus: A New Challenge

CHAPTER 9:   Personal Life: Family, Relationships, and Philanthropy

CHAPTER 10:   Legacy and Influence: Ronaldo's Impact on Football

CHAPTER 11: Turbulence and Triumph: Ups and Downs of a Legendary Career

CHAPTER 12: Beyond Football: Business Ventures and Endorsements

CHAPTER 13: The Final Act: Retirement and Reflections

Conclusion

CHAPTER 1: Early Life and Childhood

Cristiano Ronaldo dos Santos Aveiro was born on February 5, 1985, on the island of Madeira, Portugal, in the city of Funchal. He was the youngest child of Maria Dolores dos Santos Aveiro, a cook, and José Dinis Aveiro, a municipal gardener. Ronaldo grew up in a working-class family in the Santo António neighborhood, alongside his three siblings, two sisters, Elma and Liliana Cátia, and one older brother, Hugo.

From a young age, Ronaldo showed a keen interest and talent in football. He began playing at the local club Andorinha at just eight years old. Ronaldo's father, who worked as a kit man at the club, played a significant role in nurturing his son's passion for the sport. It was here that Ronaldo honed his skills and developed the athleticism and determination that would later define his career.

Ronaldo's talent soon caught the attention of scouts from Sporting Lisbon, one of Portugal's top football clubs. At the age of 12, he left his family and hometown to join Sporting's youth academy in Lisbon, where he would receive formal training and education in football. The decision to move away from home at such a young age was not easy for Ronaldo, but it was a necessary step in pursuing his dream of becoming a professional footballer.

Life in Lisbon presented its challenges for Ronaldo. He had to adapt to a new environment, away from the comfort and familiarity of his family. However, his determination and work ethic helped him overcome these obstacles. Ronaldo excelled in Sporting's youth teams, showcasing his exceptional talent and catching the eye of coaches and scouts.

In 2001, at the age of 16, Ronaldo made his professional debut for Sporting Lisbon's senior team. His performances on the field quickly drew attention from top clubs across Europe. In 2003, he caught the eye of Manchester United manager Sir Alex Ferguson during a pre-season friendly between Sporting Lisbon and Manchester United. Impressed by Ronaldo's skill, speed, and potential, Ferguson wasted no time in signing him to Manchester United in a deal worth £12.24 million, making him the most expensive teenager in English football at the time.

Ronaldo's early life and childhood experiences played a crucial role in shaping the man and player he would become. His humble beginnings instilled in him a strong work ethic, resilience, and determination to succeed against all odds. These qualities, coupled with his exceptional talent, propelled him to the pinnacle of football success and made him one of the greatest players of all time.

CHAPTER 2: Rise to Stardom: Sporting Lisbon Days

Cristiano Ronaldo's rise to stardom can be traced back to his formative years at Sporting Lisbon, where he honed his skills and caught the attention of football enthusiasts and scouts alike.

At Sporting Lisbon's youth academy, Ronaldo's exceptional talent quickly became apparent. He possessed an innate ability to dribble past opponents with ease, coupled with blistering pace and a powerful shot. Under the guidance of Sporting's coaches, Ronaldo's raw talent was refined, and he rapidly progressed through the ranks of the club's youth teams.

In 2002, Ronaldo's breakthrough moment came when he made his first-team debut for Sporting Lisbon at the tender age of 16. His performance on the field was nothing short of mesmerizing, showcasing his flair, agility, and goal-scoring prowess. Ronaldo's impact was immediate, and he soon became a regular starter for the senior team, despite his young age.

During his time at Sporting Lisbon, Ronaldo's star continued to rise. He played a key role in helping the club achieve success both domestically and in European competitions. His remarkable performances caught the eye of scouts from some of Europe's top clubs, who were eager to secure the signature of this young prodigy.

In the 2002-2003 season, Ronaldo's talent was on full display as he helped Sporting Lisbon win the Portuguese Super Cup. His electrifying pace and dazzling skills mesmerized fans and opponents alike, earning him rave reviews from pundits and coaches across the footballing world.

However, it was Ronaldo's performance in a pre-season friendly against Manchester United in 2003 that would change the course of his career. His mesmerizing display caught the eye of Manchester United manager Sir Alex Ferguson, who was determined to bring the young Portuguese sensation to Old Trafford.

In August 2003, Ronaldo completed a dream move to Manchester United, joining the club for a then-record fee for a teenager. While his departure from Sporting Lisbon was a bittersweet moment for fans, it marked the beginning of a new chapter in Ronaldo's career—one that would see him become one of the most iconic and successful footballers of his generation.

Ronaldo's time at Sporting Lisbon laid the foundation for his illustrious career. It was here that he developed the skills, mentality, and determination that would propel him to greatness on the world stage. Despite leaving the club at a young age, Ronaldo's bond with Sporting Lisbon remains strong, and he has often spoken fondly of his time at the club that helped shape him into the superstar he is today.

CHAPTER 3: Manchester United: The Making of a Global Icon

Cristiano Ronaldo's tenure at Manchester United marked a pivotal period in his career, during which he transformed from a promising talent into a global icon. Arriving at the club as a relatively unknown teenager from Sporting Lisbon in 2003, Ronaldo quickly endeared himself to fans with his electrifying style of play and insatiable hunger for success.

Under the guidance of legendary manager Sir Alex Ferguson, Ronaldo flourished at Manchester United. Ferguson recognized Ronaldo's immense potential and provided him with the platform to showcase his talent on the biggest stage. The Scot's man-management skills and tactical acumen played a crucial role in Ronaldo's development as a player and a leader.

Ronaldo's impact at Manchester United was immediate. Blessed with blistering pace, exquisite dribbling ability, and a thunderous right foot, he terrorized opposition defenses and left spectators in awe with his breathtaking performances. His partnership with Wayne Rooney and other talented teammates formed the backbone of a formidable United side that dominated English and European football during the mid-2000s.

The 2006-2007 season was a defining moment in Ronaldo's career. He enjoyed a sensational campaign, scoring 23 league goals and guiding Manchester United to their first Premier League title in four years. Ronaldo's individual brilliance earned him numerous accolades, including the PFA Players' Player of the Year and the prestigious Ballon d'Or award.

However, it was in the following season that Ronaldo truly cemented his status as a global icon. The 2007-2008 campaign saw Ronaldo reach new heights, as he played a pivotal role in Manchester United's historic treble-winning season. He scored an astonishing 42 goals in all competitions, including crucial strikes in the Premier League, FA Cup, and UEFA Champions League.

Ronaldo's crowning moment came in the Champions League final against Chelsea, where his towering header in the 26th minute opened the scoring for Manchester United. Although the match ended in a tense 1-1 draw after extra time, United emerged victorious in the penalty shootout, securing their third European Cup triumph and completing a memorable treble.

Individually, Ronaldo's stellar performances did not go unnoticed, as he claimed numerous individual awards, including his second consecutive Ballon d'Or. His mesmerizing displays on the pitch captivated audiences worldwide, and he was widely regarded as the best player in the world.

Off the field, Ronaldo's charisma and marketability transcended football, as he became a global icon and brand ambassador for numerous companies. His popularity soared, and he amassed a legion of devoted fans who admired not only his footballing prowess but also his dedication, work ethic, and philanthropy.

In June 2009, after six successful seasons at Manchester United, Ronaldo departed the club to fulfill his childhood dream of playing for Real Madrid. His time at Old Trafford had come to an end, but his legacy as one of the greatest players in Manchester United's illustrious history was firmly secured.

Ronaldo's journey from a raw talent to a global icon during his time at Manchester United serves as a testament to his unparalleled talent, determination, and relentless pursuit of excellence. His impact on the club and the Premier League remains indelible, and he will forever be remembered as one of the true greats of the game.

CHAPTER 4 : European Glory: Champions League Success

Cristiano Ronaldo's journey to European glory in the UEFA Champions League is a tale of perseverance, determination, and unparalleled skill. Throughout his illustrious career, Ronaldo has established himself as one of the competition's most iconic figures, delivering unforgettable performances on the grandest stage of European club football.

Ronaldo's first taste of Champions League success came during his time at Manchester United. In the 2007-2008 season, he played a pivotal role in guiding the Red Devils to their third European Cup triumph. Ronaldo's goal-scoring exploits were instrumental in United's journey to the final, as he netted eight goals in the tournament, including crucial strikes against Roma and Barcelona in the quarter-finals and semi-finals, respectively.

The crowning moment of Ronaldo's Champions League success with Manchester United came in the final against Chelsea. Facing their English rivals in Moscow, United battled to a 1-1 draw after extra time, with Ronaldo scoring United's opening goal with a powerful header in the first half. Although the match was ultimately decided by a dramatic penalty shootout, Ronaldo's contribution was undeniable as he played a vital role in securing the trophy for his team.

After joining Real Madrid in 2009, Ronaldo continued to dominate the Champions League stage with his new club. In the 2013-2014 season, he played a starring role in Real Madrid's historic 'La Decima' triumph, as the club lifted its 10th European Cup. Ronaldo's incredible goal-scoring form was instrumental in Madrid's success, as he netted an astonishing 17 goals in just 11 appearances, breaking the record for the most goals scored in a single Champions League campaign.

The final against Atletico Madrid saw Ronaldo deliver a match-winning performance, scoring the fourth goal in a thrilling 4-1 victory after extra time. His powerful header in the 120th minute sealed the win for Real Madrid and cemented his status as one of the greatest players in the history of the competition.

Ronaldo's Champions League success with Real Madrid continued in the following seasons, as he played a crucial role in guiding the club to three consecutive titles from 2016 to 2018. During this remarkable period, Ronaldo's extraordinary goal-scoring exploits propelled Real Madrid to unprecedented success in the modern era of the Champions League.

His performances in the knockout stages were particularly memorable, as he scored decisive goals against some of Europe's top teams, including Bayern Munich, Juventus, and Paris Saint-Germain. In the 2017-2018 season, Ronaldo's stunning bicycle kick goal against Juventus in the quarter-finals captured the imagination of football fans worldwide and epitomized his unrivaled talent and athleticism.

Ronaldo's unparalleled success in the Champions League has solidified his legacy as one of the competition's all-time greats. His ability to deliver on the biggest stage, coupled with his relentless pursuit of excellence, has set him apart as a true legend of European football. Whether wearing the colors of Manchester United, Real Madrid, or later Juventus, Ronaldo's impact on the Champions League will be remembered for generations to come.

CHAPTER 5: International Career: Portugal's Golden Boy

Cristiano Ronaldo's international career with the Portuguese national team has been nothing short of extraordinary, earning him the title of Portugal's Golden Boy. From his debut as a fresh-faced teenager to leading his country to historic triumphs, Ronaldo has left an indelible mark on the international stage, becoming one of the most decorated and revered players in the history of Portuguese football.

Ronaldo made his senior international debut for Portugal in August 2003, just weeks after joining Manchester United. Despite his young age, he showcased his immense talent and potential, providing a glimpse of what was to come in the years ahead. Over the course of his international career, Ronaldo has represented Portugal with distinction, displaying leadership, passion, and an unwavering commitment to success.

One of the defining moments of Ronaldo's international career came at the 2004 UEFA European Championship held in Portugal. Despite the disappointment of losing in the final to Greece, Ronaldo's performances throughout the tournament earned him widespread acclaim and established him as one of Europe's brightest young talents.

In the years that followed, Ronaldo continued to excel for Portugal, playing a crucial role in the team's qualification for major tournaments and leading by example on the field. His influence was particularly evident during the 2006 FIFA World Cup in Germany, where he scored his first World Cup goal against Iran and played a key role in Portugal's run to the semi-finals.

However, it was at the UEFA European Championship in 2016 that Ronaldo etched his name into Portuguese football folklore. Despite facing adversity and criticism throughout the tournament, he inspired Portugal to an unlikely triumph, as they lifted the trophy for the first time in their history. Ronaldo's leadership and resilience were on full display in the final against France, where he was forced off with injury in the first half but continued to provide guidance and motivation from the sidelines. Portugal emerged victorious thanks to an extra-time goal from Eder, securing a historic triumph and cementing Ronaldo's status as a national hero.

Ronaldo's international career has been defined by his remarkable consistency and longevity. He has shattered numerous records while wearing the Portuguese jersey, including becoming the country's all-time leading scorer and the first player to score in four consecutive European Championships. His passion for representing his country remains undiminished, as evidenced by his continued commitment to the national team well into his thirties.

In addition to his individual achievements, Ronaldo's impact on Portuguese football transcends the pitch. He has inspired a new generation of players and fans, instilling a sense of pride and belief in the country's footballing capabilities. His philanthropic efforts and charitable work off the field further underscore his dedication to making a positive difference in the lives of others.

As Portugal's Golden Boy, Cristiano Ronaldo's international career represents the epitome of excellence, determination, and success. His contributions to the national team will be remembered and celebrated for generations to come, solidifying his legacy as one of the greatest footballers of all time.

CHAPTER 6: Real Madrid Era: Records and Rivalries

Cristiano Ronaldo's tenure at Real Madrid stands as one of the most illustrious and prolific periods in the history of both the club and the player himself. Arriving at the Santiago Bernabéu in the summer of 2009, Ronaldo was tasked with the monumental challenge of filling the void left by the departure of club legend, Raúl, and delivering the coveted UEFA Champions League trophy back to the Spanish capital.

From the moment he donned the famous white jersey, Ronaldo wasted no time in making his mark on the club. His debut season saw him score an impressive 33 goals in La Liga, instantly endearing himself to the demanding Real Madrid faithful. However, it was in the subsequent seasons that Ronaldo truly ascended to a level of greatness that few players have ever reached.

Under the guidance of managers such as José Mourinho, Carlo Ancelotti, and Zinedine Zidane, Ronaldo's goal-scoring exploits reached unprecedented heights. Season after season, he continued to rewrite the record books, setting new standards for excellence in front of goal.

From his blistering pace and lethal finishing to his aerial prowess and thunderous free-kicks, Ronaldo possessed a diverse skill set that made him virtually unstoppable on the pitch.

The crowning achievement of Ronaldo's Real Madrid career came in the 2013-2014 season when he led the club to its historic 'La Decima' triumph. After a 12-year wait, Real Madrid reclaimed their status as champions of Europe, with Ronaldo playing a central role in the team's success. His 17 goals in the Champions League that season remains a record to this day, cementing his legacy as one of the competition's all-time greats.

Ronaldo's time at Real Madrid was also defined by his fierce rivalry with Barcelona's Lionel Messi. The two superstars engaged in a captivating duel for individual and team honors, pushing each other to new heights of excellence. Their meetings in El Clásico, the fiercely contested derby between Real Madrid and Barcelona, became the stuff of legend, captivating audiences around the world with their extraordinary skill and competitiveness.

Despite the intense rivalry, Ronaldo and Messi shared a mutual respect and admiration for each other's talents. Their friendly rivalry elevated both players to unprecedented levels of success and raised the bar for excellence in modern football.

In addition to his individual accolades and records, Ronaldo's time at Real Madrid was characterized by his impact on the club's success. During his nine-year spell in the Spanish capital, he helped Real Madrid capture numerous domestic and international titles, including four Champions League trophies, two La Liga titles, and several domestic cup triumphs.

Off the pitch, Ronaldo's influence extended beyond football, as he became a global icon and ambassador for the Real Madrid brand. His immense popularity and marketability made him one of the most recognizable and influential athletes in the world, transcending the sport and reaching audiences far beyond the confines of the football pitch.

In July 2018, after nine unforgettable seasons at Real Madrid, Ronaldo embarked on a new chapter in his career, joining Italian giants Juventus. His departure marked the end of an era at the Santiago Bernabéu, but his legacy as one of the greatest players in the history of Real Madrid and world football will endure for generations to come. Ronaldo's time at Real Madrid was defined by records, rivalries, and relentless pursuit of excellence, leaving an indelible mark on the club and the sport as a whole.

CHAPTER 7: Ballon d'Or Dominance: Individual Accolades

Cristiano Ronaldo's dominance in the race for the Ballon d'Or, football's most prestigious individual award, is a testament to his unparalleled talent, dedication, and longevity at the highest level of the sport. Over the course of his illustrious career, Ronaldo has amassed a record number of Ballon d'Or titles, firmly establishing himself as one of the greatest players in the history of the game.

Ronaldo's first Ballon d'Or triumph came in 2008, following his remarkable performances for Manchester United during the 2007-2008 season. His role in guiding United to a Premier League and UEFA Champions League double, coupled with his electrifying displays on the pitch, made him a deserving recipient of football's most prestigious individual accolade. At the age of 23, Ronaldo became the first Portuguese player to win the Ballon d'Or since its inception in 1956, signaling his arrival among the elite players in the world.

Following his move to Real Madrid in 2009, Ronaldo continued to assert his dominance on the global stage, capturing the hearts of fans and pundits alike with his mesmerizing skill and goal-scoring prowess. In 2013, he claimed his second Ballon d'Or title after a sensational season that saw him break numerous records, including setting a new mark for the most goals scored in a single Champions League campaign.

Ronaldo's Ballon d'Or dominance reached new heights in 2014, as he secured his third title following another stellar campaign with Real Madrid. His remarkable goal-scoring feats, which included netting 17 goals in the

Champions League alone, propelled him to the pinnacle of individual success once again, solidifying his status as one of the greatest players of his generation.

In 2016, Ronaldo added a fourth Ballon d'Or to his collection, capping off a memorable year that saw him lead Portugal to an improbable triumph at the UEFA European Championship. His leadership and heroics on the international stage, coupled with his outstanding performances for Real Madrid, made him the clear choice for football's top individual honor.

Ronaldo's Ballon d'Or dominance continued in 2017, as he claimed his fifth title following another stellar season with Real Madrid. His role in guiding the club to a historic Champions League triumph, coupled with his prolific goal-scoring form, reaffirmed his status as one of the sport's all-time greats.

Throughout his career, Ronaldo's relentless pursuit of excellence and unwavering commitment to success have set him apart from his peers. His ability to perform at the highest level year after year, coupled with his unparalleled work ethic and determination, have made him a deserving recipient of football's most prestigious individual award on multiple occasions.

Off the pitch, Ronaldo's influence extends far beyond football, as he has become a global icon and ambassador for the sport. His immense popularity and marketability have helped raise the profile of football to new heights, inspiring millions of fans around the world and leaving an indelible mark on the game.

As Ronaldo continues to defy the odds and push the boundaries of what is possible on the football pitch, his legacy as one of the greatest players in the history of the sport is secure. His Ballon d'Or dominance serves as a testament to his unparalleled talent, dedication, and enduring impact on the world of football.

CHAPTER 8: Transfer to Juventus: A New Challenge

Cristiano Ronaldo's transfer to Juventus in the summer of 2018 marked a significant milestone in his illustrious career, as he embarked on a new challenge in Serie A after nine successful seasons at Real Madrid. The move to the Italian giants was met with widespread anticipation and excitement, as football fans around the world eagerly awaited the prospect of seeing one of the game's greatest players ply his trade in a new league and environment.

Ronaldo's decision to join Juventus came as a surprise to many, signaling his desire for a fresh challenge and new opportunities to test himself at the highest level. Despite enjoying unprecedented success at Real Madrid, including four Champions League titles and numerous domestic honors, Ronaldo remained hungry for further achievements and felt that Juventus offered the ideal platform to continue his pursuit of excellence.

Upon his arrival in Turin, Ronaldo was greeted with a hero's welcome, as Juventus supporters flocked to the Allianz Stadium to catch a glimpse of their new talisman. The anticipation surrounding his debut was palpable, with fans and pundits alike eager to see how he would adapt to the rigors of Italian football and make his mark on Serie A.

Ronaldo's impact at Juventus was immediate, as he wasted no time in showcasing his immense talent and goal-scoring prowess. In his first season with the club, he played a central role in guiding Juventus to their eighth consecutive Serie A title, finishing as the team's top scorer with 21 league goals. His leadership on and off the pitch was instrumental in helping Juventus maintain their dominance in Italian football and cementing his status as a fan favorite among the Bianconeri faithful.

In addition to his domestic success, Ronaldo also made his presence felt in the UEFA Champions League, where he played a key role in Juventus' run to the quarter-finals. His memorable hat-trick against Atletico Madrid in the round of 16 was a testament to his ability to deliver on the biggest stage and inspired Juventus to a remarkable comeback victory.

Off the pitch, Ronaldo's arrival at Juventus had a transformative effect on the club's global profile and commercial appeal. His immense popularity and marketability helped attract new sponsors and partnerships, while his presence in Turin generated unprecedented interest and excitement among fans and media alike.

Despite facing challenges and setbacks along the way, including changes in management and competition from rival clubs, Ronaldo remained steadfast in his commitment to Juventus and his pursuit of success. His relentless work ethic, dedication, and winning mentality served as a source of inspiration for his teammates and a driving force behind the club's continued success on the domestic front.

As Ronaldo continues to ply his trade at Juventus, his transfer to the club represents more than just a new chapter in his career—it symbolizes his unyielding determination to push the boundaries of what is possible and achieve greatness wherever he goes. Whether it's breaking records, winning titles, or inspiring the next generation of footballers, Ronaldo's impact at Juventus will be felt for years to come, cementing his legacy as one of the greatest players of all time.

CHAPTER 9: Personal Life: Family, Relationships, and Philanthropy

Cristiano Ronaldo's personal life is a story of family, relationships, and philanthropy that complements his illustrious football career. Despite the glare of the spotlight, Ronaldo has maintained a strong connection to his roots and prioritized the well-being of his loved ones, while also using his platform for charitable endeavors and social causes.

Family has always been central to Ronaldo's life, providing him with a foundation of love and support throughout his journey to footballing greatness. He shares a close bond with his mother, Maria Dolores dos Santos Aveiro, who has been a constant source of encouragement and inspiration. Ronaldo's upbringing on the island of Madeira instilled in him a strong sense of family values, which he continues to cherish to this day.

In addition to his mother, Ronaldo's relationship with his siblings—sisters Elma and Liliana Cátia, and brother Hugo—has played an important role in shaping his identity and character.

Despite the demands of his career and global fame, Ronaldo has remained deeply connected to his family, regularly sharing moments of joy and celebration with them both on and off the pitch.

Ronaldo's personal life has also been marked by high-profile relationships with partners such as Russian model Irina Shayk and Spanish model Georgina Rodríguez. His relationship with Rodríguez, whom he met in 2016, has been particularly significant, with the couple welcoming several children together and forming a tight-knit family unit.

Fatherhood has brought a new dimension to Ronaldo's life, allowing him to experience the joys and responsibilities of parenthood firsthand. He is the proud father of four children—Cristiano Jr., twins Eva and Mateo, and daughter Alana Martina—all of whom hold a special place in his heart. Ronaldo's dedication to his children is evident in his social media posts and public appearances, where he often shares tender moments and expressions of paternal love.

Beyond his personal relationships, Ronaldo's philanthropic efforts have made a meaningful impact on communities around the world. Through his CR7 Foundation, he has supported numerous charitable initiatives focused on children's education, health, and well-being. Ronaldo's foundation has funded schools, hospitals, and sports facilities in countries such as Portugal, Mozambique, and Nepal, providing opportunities for disadvantaged youth to thrive and succeed.

In addition to his foundation work, Ronaldo has also been involved in various charitable campaigns and fundraising efforts, using his platform to raise awareness and support for causes close to his heart. From donating blood to supporting disaster relief efforts, Ronaldo has demonstrated a commitment to giving back and making a positive difference in the world.

In summary, Cristiano Ronaldo's personal life is a testament to the values of family, love, and compassion that define him as both a football icon and a human being. Whether spending time with his loved ones, supporting charitable causes, or inspiring others through his actions, Ronaldo continues to leave a lasting legacy that extends far beyond the confines of the football pitch.

CHAPTER 10: Legacy and Influence: Ronaldo's Impact on Football

Cristiano Ronaldo's legacy and influence on football extend far beyond his remarkable achievements on the pitch. Throughout his illustrious career, Ronaldo has left an indelible mark on the sport, shaping its evolution and inspiring millions of fans around the world. From his unparalleled skill and athleticism to his relentless work ethic and dedication,

Ronaldo's impact on football transcends generations and continents.

At the heart of Ronaldo's legacy is his extraordinary talent and ability to perform at the highest level consistently. Renowned for his blistering pace, impeccable technique, and lethal finishing, Ronaldo possesses a diverse skill set that has revolutionized the way the game is played. Whether scoring goals with his head, feet, or even his chest, Ronaldo's versatility and creativity have made him a nightmare for opposition defenders and a joy to watch for fans of all ages.

Ronaldo's influence on the modern game can be seen in his innovative playing style and relentless pursuit of excellence. His commitment to physical fitness, diet, and recovery methods has set new standards for professional athletes, inspiring a generation of players to prioritize their health and well-being. Ronaldo's relentless work ethic and dedication to self-improvement have become a blueprint for success, motivating aspiring footballers to push themselves to new heights in pursuit of their dreams.

Off the pitch, Ronaldo's impact on football extends beyond his performances on the field. As one of the most marketable athletes in the world, he has helped raise the profile of the sport to unprecedented levels, attracting new fans and commercial partners from around the globe. Ronaldo's immense popularity on social media platforms has given him a platform to connect with fans on a personal level, providing insights into his life and career that were previously inaccessible.

Ronaldo's influence on football culture can also be seen in his transcendent status as a global icon and brand ambassador. From his signature celebration to his iconic CR7 brand, Ronaldo's image is synonymous with excellence, success, and glamor. His appeal transcends borders and cultures, resonating with fans of all backgrounds and nationalities, and helping to bridge divides in an increasingly interconnected world.

Beyond his individual achievements, Ronaldo's impact on football is also evident in his role as a mentor and role model for the next generation of players. Through his actions on and off the pitch, he has demonstrated the values of hard work, perseverance, and sportsmanship, inspiring young athletes to strive for greatness and pursue their passions with unwavering dedication.

As Cristiano Ronaldo's illustrious career enters its twilight years, his legacy as one of the greatest players in the history of football is secure. His impact on the sport will be felt for generations to come, shaping the way it is played, perceived, and celebrated around the world. Ronaldo's influence extends far beyond the confines of the football pitch, leaving an indelible mark on the sport and inspiring millions to dream, believe, and achieve greatness.

CHAPTER 11: Turbulence and Triumph: Ups and Downs of a Legendary Career

Cristiano Ronaldo's legendary career has been characterized by both turbulence and triumph, as he navigated through a series of ups and downs on his journey to footballing greatness. From early setbacks and challenges to historic achievements and moments of glory, Ronaldo's career is a testament to resilience, determination, and unwavering belief in his abilities.

Ronaldo's journey to the pinnacle of football began in Madeira, Portugal, where he overcame humble beginnings and financial struggles to pursue his passion for the game. From a young age, Ronaldo displayed an extraordinary talent for football, catching the eye of scouts and coaches with his raw skill and athleticism. However, his path to success was not without obstacles, as he faced skepticism and doubts from critics who questioned whether he had what it takes to succeed at the highest level.

Despite the challenges, Ronaldo remained undeterred in his pursuit of greatness, channeling his setbacks into motivation and fueling his desire to prove his detractors wrong. His breakthrough came at Sporting Lisbon, where he honed his skills and caught the attention of top European clubs with his dazzling performances on the pitch. In 2003, Ronaldo made the leap to Manchester United, marking the beginning of a new chapter in his career.

Ronaldo's time at Manchester United was marked by both triumph and adversity, as he endured criticism and scrutiny while also achieving unprecedented success on the field. His early years at the club were characterized by flashes of brilliance and moments of inconsistency, as he adapted to the physicality and intensity of the

Premier League. However, under the guidance of Sir Alex Ferguson, Ronaldo flourished, developing into one of the most feared and revered players in world football.

In 2008, Ronaldo reached the pinnacle of his career at Manchester United, leading the club to a historic Premier League and Champions League double and winning his first Ballon d'Or award. His individual and collective success at United solidified his status as one of the best players in the world and set the stage for a record-breaking move to Real Madrid in 2009.

Ronaldo's transfer to Real Madrid marked a new chapter in his career, as he embarked on a quest to conquer new challenges and achieve even greater success in the Spanish capital. Despite facing pressure and expectations, Ronaldo thrived at Real Madrid, becoming the club's all-time leading scorer and guiding them to multiple domestic and international titles, including four Champions League trophies.

However, Ronaldo's time at Real Madrid was not without its share of turbulence. He faced criticism and scrutiny from fans and media alike, endured injury setbacks, and experienced moments of frustration and disappointment. Despite the challenges, Ronaldo remained resolute in his pursuit of excellence, using adversity as fuel to propel himself to even greater heights.

In 2018, Ronaldo embarked on a new chapter in his career, joining Juventus in search of fresh challenges and opportunities for success. His move to the Italian giants was met with anticipation and excitement, as fans eagerly awaited the prospect of seeing one of the game's greatest players ply his trade in Serie A. Despite facing skepticism and doubts, Ronaldo embraced the challenge head-on, quickly establishing himself as a key player for

Juventus and leading the club to domestic success.

Throughout his legendary career, Ronaldo's ability to overcome adversity and triumph in the face of adversity has been a defining characteristic. Whether facing criticism, injury, or personal setbacks, Ronaldo has always risen to the occasion, demonstrating resilience, determination, and a relentless pursuit of excellence. His journey from humble beginnings to footballing greatness is a testament to the power of perseverance and the belief that anything is possible with hard work, dedication, and unwavering self-belief.

CHAPTER 12: Beyond Football: Business Ventures and Endorsements

Beyond his incredible achievements on the football pitch, Cristiano Ronaldo has leveraged his global fame and marketability to build a successful portfolio of business ventures and endorsements. From fashion and fragrance to technology and hospitality, Ronaldo's entrepreneurial spirit and keen business acumen have propelled him to success off the field, establishing him as one of the most influential and marketable athletes in the world.

One of Ronaldo's most notable business ventures is his CR7 brand, which encompasses a wide range of products and services, including clothing, footwear, fragrance, and accessories. Launched in 2006 in collaboration with various partners and designers, the CR7 brand reflects Ronaldo's personal style and ethos, blending sophistication, elegance, and athleticism into a cohesive and aspirational lifestyle brand.

The CR7 brand has enjoyed widespread success, with its clothing and footwear lines appealing to a diverse and global audience of fans and fashion enthusiasts. Ronaldo's involvement in the design and promotion of the brand has helped it resonate with consumers and establish a strong presence in the competitive fashion industry. From sleek suits and casual wear to stylish sneakers and accessories, the CR7 brand offers something for everyone, reflecting Ronaldo's versatility and broad appeal.

In addition to his clothing and fragrance lines, Ronaldo has also ventured into the world of technology and digital media, partnering with leading brands and companies to launch innovative products and services. He has collaborated with companies such as Nike, Samsung, and

PokerStars to develop signature merchandise, digital campaigns, and interactive experiences that engage fans and consumers across various platforms.

Ronaldo's endorsement deals and sponsorship agreements have further bolstered his business empire, with brands eager to align themselves with his image and global appeal. He has served as a brand ambassador for companies such as Coca-Cola, Herbalife, and Clear Men, lending his name and likeness to advertising campaigns and promotional initiatives around the world. Ronaldo's endorsement deals have not only enriched his own coffers but have also generated significant revenue and exposure for the brands he represents.

Beyond his business ventures and endorsements, Ronaldo has also demonstrated a commitment to philanthropy and social responsibility, using his platform and resources to make a positive impact on the world. Through his CR7 Foundation, he has supported numerous charitable initiatives focused on children's education, health, and well-being, funding schools, hospitals, and sports facilities in countries around the world. Ronaldo's philanthropic efforts have earned him praise and admiration from fans and peers alike, further enhancing his reputation as a role model and humanitarian.

In summary, Cristiano Ronaldo's success off the football pitch is a testament to his entrepreneurial spirit, business savvy, and commitment to excellence in all endeavors. Through his CR7 brand, endorsement deals, and philanthropic initiatives, Ronaldo has built a diverse and lucrative business empire that extends far beyond the confines of the football pitch. As he continues to expand his business ventures and make a positive impact on the world, Ronaldo's influence and legacy will endure for generations to come.

CHAPTER 13: The Final Act: Retirement and Reflections

Cristiano Ronaldo's retirement from professional football will mark the culmination of an illustrious career that has spanned over two decades and left an indelible mark on the sport. As one of the greatest players in the history of football, Ronaldo's final act on the pitch will be a momentous occasion, prompting reflections on his legacy, achievements, and impact on the game.

Throughout his career, Ronaldo has dazzled fans around the world with his extraordinary talent, athleticism, and goal-scoring prowess. From his early days as a prodigious talent at Sporting Lisbon to his record-breaking spells at Manchester United, Real Madrid, and Juventus, Ronaldo has consistently pushed the boundaries of what is possible on the football pitch, setting new standards of excellence and inspiring generations of players to follow in his footsteps.

As Ronaldo prepares to hang up his boots, he leaves behind a legacy that is unparalleled in the annals of football history. With five Ballon d'Or awards, numerous league titles, and four UEFA Champions League trophies to his name, Ronaldo's list of accolades speaks volumes about his impact on the game and his enduring legacy as one of the all-time greats.

Beyond his individual achievements, Ronaldo's influence on football extends far beyond the confines of the pitch. As a global icon and ambassador for the sport, he has helped elevate football to unprecedented levels of popularity and commercial success, attracting new fans and followers from around the world and transcending cultural and geographic boundaries.

Ronaldo's retirement will also prompt reflections on his personal journey and the sacrifices he made along the way to achieve greatness. From his humble beginnings in Madeira to the glitz and glamor of the world's biggest clubs, Ronaldo's rise to superstardom has been marked by perseverance, determination, and unwavering self-belief. His journey serves as a reminder that success is not achieved overnight but is the result of hard work, dedication, and a relentless pursuit of excellence.

As Ronaldo bids farewell to the game he has graced for so many years, he leaves behind a legacy that will endure for generations to come. His impact on football, both on and off the pitch, will be felt for years to come, as he continues to inspire players, fans, and aspiring athletes around the world to dream big and never give up on their goals.

In retirement, Ronaldo will have the opportunity to reflect on his incredible journey and the memories he has created along the way. From unforgettable goals and historic victories to moments of triumph and adversity, Ronaldo's career has been a rollercoaster ride of emotions and experiences that have shaped him into the person and player he is today.

As he embarks on the next chapter of his life, Ronaldo will undoubtedly continue to make a difference in the world, whether through his philanthropic endeavors, business ventures, or contributions to the sport he loves. His legacy as one of the greatest footballers of all time is secure, but perhaps more importantly, Ronaldo leaves behind a legacy of inspiration, resilience, and unwavering determination that will continue to inspire generations to come.

CONCLUSION

Cristiano Ronaldo's journey from a young talent in Madeira to a global footballing icon has been nothing short of extraordinary. With his unparalleled skill, relentless work ethic, and unwavering determination, Ronaldo has left an indelible mark on the sport, inspiring millions around the world. As he embarks on the next chapter of his life, Ronaldo's legacy as one of the greatest players of all time is secure, but his impact on football and beyond will continue to resonate for generations to come.

Made in the USA
Columbia, SC
08 August 2024

40144385R00048